MESSERSCHMITT ME 262
VOL. II

THE WORLD'S FIRST TURBOJET FIGHTER

Manfred Griehl

SCHIFFER MILITARY HISTORY

West Chester, PA

Sources:
Allied ADIK Reports
Factory Data, Messerschmitt AG
Factory Data, Junkers AG
Files and Reports of the Luftwaffe High Command (OKL),
Quartermaster General

Photos:

Bekker Collection (6)
Dabrowski Collection (3)
Heck Collection (4)
Jayne Collection (6)
Grimminger Collection (2)
Holzmann Collection (1)
Air Archives (11)
Lutz Collection (12)
Marchand Collection (1)

MBB Archives (4)
Muth Collection (3)
Nowarra Collection (3)
NASM, Washington DC (2)
Petrick Collection (4)
Selinger Collection (1)
Author's archives
Podzun-Pallas archives

Translated from the German by Edward Force.

Printed in the United States of America.
ISBN: 0-88740-410-3

This title was originally published under the title,
Me 262 - Das Vielzweckflugzeug, 2. Band,
by Podzun-Pallas Verlag, Friedberg.

We are interested in hearing from authors with book ideas on related topics. We are also looking for good photographs in the military history area. We will copy your photos and credit you should your materials be used in a future Schiffer project.

Published by Schiffer Publishing, Ltd.
1469 Morstein Road
West Chester, Pennsylvania 19380
Please write for a free catalog.
This book may be purchased from the publisher.
Please include $2.00 postage.
Try your bookstore first.

Three planes of *Erprobungskommando* (Test Command) 262 at Lechfeld, summer 1944.

Me 262 - Multipurpose Aircraft

Development

One of the most important eras of aircraft building began towards the end of the 1930s.

The Messerschmitt AG began with the concept of the subsequent Me 262, then still designated Project (P) 65. Practical testing began as of April 1941. After the rigidity of the P 1065 cell was proved, the first test engines could be installed. By the summer of 1942, five prototypes with BMW 003 turbines had been planned. Because of their insufficient technical development, Jumo 004 engines had to be used instead for a time. In August 1942, the number of test models was increased to ten to speed up development. When the Reich Air Ministry was finally convinced of the jet planes' high performance, *Feldmarschall* Erhard Milch halted production of the Me 209 on May 25, 1943 and simultaneously ordered the prompt series production of the Me 262, which was planned as a multipurpose aircraft.

By May of 1943, despite all efforts, only four test planes with a tail wheel were available, and even they were not all available all the time. The lacking six Me 262's were to follow as soon as possible.

In order to test the tactical aspects of its flying characteristics, the Luftwaffe High Command (OKL) — in conjunction with the Command of Test Centers (KdE) and the *General der Jagdflieger* (GdJ) — set up Test Command (*Erprobungskommando*) 262 (EKdo Lechfeld). It was led by the experienced pilot and Knight's Cross holder, *Hauptmann* Thierfelder, and stationed at Lechfeld. Messerschmitt factory pilots, using the newly delivered Me 262 V6 and V7, carried out the extensive performance testing. At the same time, the Junkers turbines were further refined and tested.

The Me 262 V3 takes off from the factory airfield in Augsburg.

Test plane Me 262 A-1a, factory number 130167.

As a result of numerous technical difficulties, as well as several crashes and wrecks, new delays continued. The beginning of the pre-series (zero series) could not be scheduled before the end of 1943. Thus the first Me 262 S (factory #130006) did not fly until March 1944.

Enemy attacks on the manufacturing plants in Augsburg and Regensburg also delayed production of the zero series. Production was then postponed until the end of March or the beginning of April 1944. In addition, test flights were disrupted considerably by a bomb attack on Leipheim.

To intensify testing and finally provide the test command with sufficient planes, the first five production planes were assembled by the Luftwaffe and the manufacturers themselves. Only then could test flying begin.

Above: Me 262 V3 at Lechfeld.

Above: Results of an air raid on Lechfeld.

Below: Crash-landing of the third production plane.

Below: The tenth production Me 262.

The "blitz bomber" with two SC 250 bombs, factory #110813.

THE BLITZ AND SCHNELL BOMBERS

To this day it is assumed by many that in 1944 Hitler, from one day to the next, ordered that the Me 262 be made into a bomber. But the truth looked very different then and still does today. In March of 1943 he had already spoken of the necessity of being able to turn every fighter plane, when necessary, into a bomber quickly. On the basis of these instructions, the aircraft manufacturers began to develop their fighters as fighter-bombers too. Why should the situation be different for the Me 262?

On November 2, 1943, Professor Messerschmitt stated that bomb bays were already planned for the Me 262. Two weeks later — when the newest airplanes were displayed at Insterburg — he again assured Hitler that the plane could be adapted as a high-speed bomber. The appropriate directions for modifying the Me 262 as a highest-speed fighter had already been submitted to the Air Ministry.

The final decision as to whether to make the jet a fighter or a bomber was put off at first, though. Only on December 5, 1943 did *Reichsmarschall* Göring proclaim Hitler's express wish for high-speed fighters that could turn back the expected invasion. Four months later, when only a few production planes had been assembled, Milch was instructed to proceed with the development of the Me 262 as a fighter only as a sideline. The "blitz bomber" now received the highest priority!

Above: A blitz bomber of *Kommando Schenk*.

Upper right: A blitz bomber being loaded with
SC bombs.

Right: The "Viking ship" bomb holders of the
Me 262 blitz bomber.

But before the first Me 262 planes reached
Rechlin-Lärz on June 10, 1944 for bomber testing,
the invasion was already in full swing. The
retraining of the KG 51 crews came more than ten
days too late. And any other decision would have
been useless. The few blitz bombers, serving as
fighters, probably could not have turned back the
invasion.

On July 26, an extensive discussion took place,
during which Hitler said: "The situation demands
fighters and still more fighters, as well as blitz
bombers like the Ar 234 and the Me 262."

Four days later, all heavy warplanes were
discontinued. To be able to fly bombing missions
over northern France — despite the Allied air
superiority — the decision remained in favor of
blitz bombers.

As of August 1944, though, every twentieth Me 262 was being used as a pure fighter. According to an announcement of its utility as a fighter (on September 12, 1944) and the only moderate combat success of *Kommando Schenk*, as of September 20 the emphasis was again placed on the fighter.

Three months before that, the often-cited "blitz bomber decision" having just become known in all its stringency, a conference of the Air Ministry, the Luftwaffe and the manufacturers took place. The path to the high-speed bomber was to have three steps:

a) Makeshift bombers with two electric carriers for cylindrical loads (ETC), without bombsights,
b) Blitz bombers (with two ETC, BZA bombsight aggregates, and TSA low-lever bombing systems,
c) Two-seat highest-speed bombers (with Lotfe systems).

Based on the experiences gained with the makeshift bomber, the first model of which was the Me 262 S10, work on production blitz bombers began in November. Tests with the first model (factory number 130170) showed a speed loss of almost 75 kph. The new blitz bomber with two SC 250 explosive bombs slung underneath could only attain 730 kph.

Above: Me 262 A-2a of KG 51.

Left: Two blitz bombers of KG 51, seen at Fassberg after the war ended.

Along with the tests of the Me 262 A-2a (the "a" indicates the Jumo engine), many tests of the jet plane's weapons were undertaken. The combined use of an Ar 234 with Hs 293 glider bombs and an Me 262A as a lead plane was considered. The composite "Mistletoe" arrangement of two Me 262 A-1/2 planes, one atop the other, with a take-off weight of over 17,000 kilograms, never took concrete form either.

Only the highest-speed bomber (SB), originally Me 262 A-3 and later called A-2a/U2, became reality. Several months after the discussion on July 15, 1944, the Me 262 A-2, factory #110484, was fitted with a glass fuselage nose for the bombardier. The first bomb drops, such as those of December 5, 1944, were held over lakes in Upper Bavaria and brought good results. Early in 1945 a second model plane was completed. This craft, factory #110555, was already equipped with the planned Siemens navigational system and various measuring devices. After 23 flights, this Me 262 crashed near Marburg on the Lahn on March 30, 1945.

Above: The cockpit of an Me 262 A-1a with additional instruments.

Left: Two Me 262's, one of them a high-speed bomber (Me 262 A-2a), are towed by an Opel Blitz tank truck.

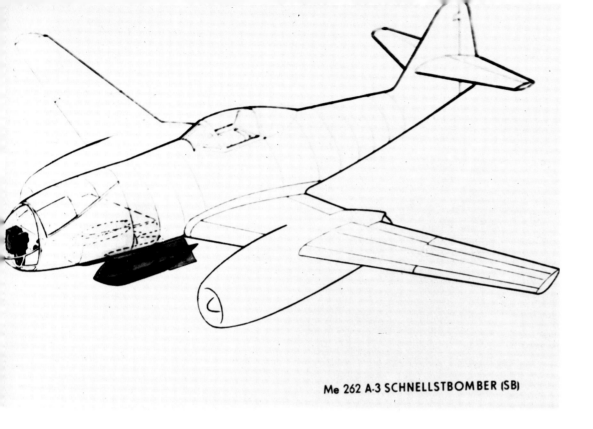

Me 262 A-3 SCHNELLSTBOMBER (SB)

Left: Drawing of the planned Me 262 A-3 highest-speed bomber (corresponding to A-2a/ U2).

Lower left: V 555 after crash-landing near Marburg.

Below: V 555 is removed by Allied troops.

Left: Aerial view of the Giebelstadt
combat air base, March 22, 1945.

Right: A direct hit on the take-off
runway at Giebelstadt.

THE BLITZ BOMBER IN KG 51

Two weeks after the invasion of Normandy, the retraining of KG 51 pilots for the Me 262 blitz bomber began. The first planes, equipped with two ETC sets, could only be made ready on July 19, 1944.

The first jet bombers were all turned over to the *Kommando Schenk,* which was formed of parts of KG 51. After relatively brief training, the pilots were then supposed to disrupt Allied supply lines with these planes. This undertaking could never be carried out with only a dozen Me 262's, several of which were put out of action during ferrying to Chateaudun. Although the pilots went into combat as often as possible, dropping bombs horizontally from several thousand meters up, most of the bombs landed far from their targets. The most sensible solution would have been to have the pilots make low-level or gliding attacks, but these were expressly forbidden.

Above:
A blitz bomber of
Kommando Schenk.

Left:
This Me 262 A-1a was found
without engines.

Meanwhile, the Allied units in northern France were pushing further and further to the east. The command post had to be moved often, finally to the Rheine area. In addition, the American and British fighters took their toll. Numerous Me 262 jets were shot down or damaged while taking off or landing.

The order to attack below 4000 meters was finally given late in the autumn of 1944. This brought a dramatic rise in combat success. Early in December of 1944 the pilots of *Kommando Schenk* were once again integrated into the I./KG 51, passing on to their colleagues the knowledge that they had gained in their first missions. At the end of 1944 the gruppe already had 42 blitz bombers, which provided decisive air support for the Ardennes offensive and Operation "Bodenplatte."

In the spring of 1945, parts of the squadron were transferred to Giebelstadt to attack targets in Alsace and later in the Hunsrück and the Rhine Valley. On February 14, 1945 there were four united attacks, each with 35-40 blitz bombers. More than 280 SC 250 bombs were dropped on Allied positions, taking a heavy toll. On February 25, 1945 as well, several high-speed bombers, this time in company with 136 piston-engine fighters, went into battle.

The *Kowalewski Gefechtverband* (Battle Squadron) was organized in mid-March of 1945 out of parts of KG 51 and KG 76. It saw service successfully in the west in the first days of April. Missions of the II./KG 51 could be carried out only to a limited extent because of fuel and engine shortages. The number of combat-ready planes sank steadily, since no more spare parts were delivered.

The last combat-ready blitz bombers were finally turned over to the Galland Fighter Unit (JV 44). A small group flew combat missions on the eastern front until the war ended.

The Neuburg-Zell air base after being bombed by the 15th U. S. Air Force.

Above: This Me 262 was captured at Fassberg and then tested in Britain.

Above: Me 262 A-1a/Bo, an interesting showpiece for the GI's.

Below: Factory #500079 at Giebelstadt on April 4, 1945.

Below: The same plane with raised engine cover.

Above: Assembling the fuselage and wings outdoors.

Below: The first Me 262 captured intact by the Allies.

Above: This jet plane was not destined for delivery.

Below: This Me 262 was destroyed on the Ulm-Munich Autobahn by low-flying enemy planes.

15

Kampfgeschwadern in Action

After the offensive bombings in the west had almost ceased to bring any success, the pilots began to be retrained for fighter combat.

The change of KG 40 to a fighter squadron was to begin in the autumn of 1944. The process moved slowly, though, because of heavy air raids, especially on Neuburg on the Danube.

For the pilots of KG 54, this new action began in August of 1944, with Fw 190 aircraft. The Me 262 arrived later. The KG(J) (J = Fighters) 54 was then the only Luftwaffe unit to attack and break up Allied packs in closed action. The final defeat was to be faced along with the piston-engine fighters.

Because the Me 262's arrived too late, the first combat mission did not take place until February 9, 1945. Unfortunately, it encountered the fighters of the 55th Fighter Group. The *Kommodore* and some of his men did not return from the battle. *Major* Bätcher took command shortly thereafter. Constant low-level attacks and numerous crashes with the unfamiliar controls prevented the I./KG(J) 54 from being ready for combat until March 5. A heavy air raid on Giebelstadt turned the air base there into a cratered landscape. After another bombing on March 24, 1945 the group had to be transferred to central Germany. There it saw its first successful action against four-engine bombers on March 25, along with planes of JG 7.

But on April 9 the unit's history hit a low point. Seventeen of the KG(J) 54's twenty-one Me 262's were lost in aerial battle or accidents.

The remainder of the unit was transferred to the Prague area in mid-April and flew fighter and other combat missions from there until the war ended.

Oberstleutnant Volprecht Riedesel, Baron von Eisenbach, Kommodore of KG(J) 54, was shot down on February 9, 1945.

Planes of the III./KG(J) 54 in take-off position at the Neuburg air base.

The low-level attacks against Soviet units and positions had a particularly demoralizing effect. The last missions were carried out in early May of 1945; then the J2 fuel was used up. The squadron received a total of 145 Me 262 planes, some of which were turned over to the II. and III. Gruppen for training.

KG 55 flew fighter missions with Bf 109 G-10 and K-4 as well as Fw 190 planes since mid-September of 1944. Later they made low-level attacks on the advancing Allies. When their fuel ran out, the "Greif" (Griffin) Battle Group was formed. The squadron received no more Me 262's.

Some of the jet fighters were turned over to KG 6. While the I./KG(J) 6 was still training with Bf 109 G-6/10/14 planes, pilots of the III./KG(J) 6 were getting acquainted with the Me 262. Along with pilots of the *Hogeback Gefechtsverband*, they saw action over Bohemia and the eastern front in the last days of the war.

Kampfgeschwadern 27 and 30 also received Bf 109 G-10, K-4 and Fw 190 A-9 planes as of October 1944, as well as a few Doras, but the promised Me 262's went to other units.

Oberleutnant Heinz Rall, *Staffelkäpitan* of III./KG(J) 54, in February, 1945.

Me 262 A-1a (B3+GR) of KG(J) 54 before take-off.

Oberfeldwebel Gentzsch was the flight instructor of III./KG(J) 54. Note the white stripe below the cockpit and the painted nose.

Above: The Messerschmitt factory at Regensburg after being bombed by the Allies.

Below: The morning after the air raid: Erding, April 18, 1945.

The woodland factory at Obertraubing. After the factories were destroyed, a new start was made here.

American soldiers found this damaged Me 262 A-1 near the Autobahn to Munich.

PRODUCTION

Only after the establishment of the *Jägerstab* (Fighter Staff) did production of the Me 262 begin in March of 1944. Against vigorous opposition, a rigorous simplification of types took place. Instead of 67 models with 578 versions, only fifteen models went into production.

The mistrust of new technology, especially that of the jet plane, caused problems for a long time. In addition, Allied air raids on the Messerschmitt factories and the test facilities at Lechfeld (December 13-16, 1943) delayed delivery of the jet fighters. The great shortage of capable workers also caused problems. Thus it was only in July of 1944 that a noteworthy number of Me 262's were ready for action. There were 28 planes, which were used to set up a test command.

With the beginning of series production, many small and medium-sized businesses became involved in the production program. The production of the Heinkel He 162 "Volksjäger" almost brought about a decrease in manufacturing.

But since the Fighter Staff was strongly in favor of the Me 262, it was possible to increase production steadily. This is shown by the fact that 101 Me 262's were built in November 1944. By the end of 1944, a total of 430 Me 262's had been produced, and 186 of them had been delivered to the Luftwaffe. All the rest were held in reserve or could not be finished yet. Production reached its high point in the spring of 1945. At that time the factories had to be vacated because of steady bomb attacks. The makeshift "moor culture" and "forest assembly" plants came into being.

In all, 1400 Me 262's may have been built, 809 of which reached the Luftwaffe.

American bombers attack the Messerschmitt factory at Augsburg, as seen from the air.

"Forest assembly" — thus did Allied soldiers find the well-camouflaged woodland assembly sites.

Training Version

The new technology of jet propulsion immediately demanded a suitable two-seat training plane. On April 23, 1943 the technicians of German Lufthansa in Berlin-Staaken set about to rebuild sixty A-1a planes.

The model, which was the fifth production plane (factory #130010), was equipped with a second seat, dual controls and modified tanks. What with the Allied invasion of Normandy, though, the Luftwaffe required every available Me 262 for combat use. There was little left for use as training planes. Thus only four trainers could be rebuilt by the Lufthansa and some fifteen by Blohm & Voss in Wenzendorf. A severe air raid on the rebuilding facilities in Wenzendorf on January 7, 1945 brought a final end to the work on the Me 262 B-1a. Only two two-seat versions left the factory after that date.

So training at EKG 1 and EJG 2 was generally limited to production Me 262 A-1a or A-2a planes. The only unit that had a significant number of jet planes for use in training was the III.(Erg.)/JG 2 at Lechfeld, the leadership of which was assumed by *Major* Heinz Bär in the spring of 1945.

The lack of training planes meant that the flight trainees went directly from theoretical schooling to the combat plane. The flight instructors could do nothing but give them instructions. This explains the numerous accidents and crashes. Retraining was ended after only eight to ten flights. Everything else was left to the combat unit. The training personnel also flew combat missions. *Major* Bär began his series of scores with the Me 262 on March 19, 1945. The last of his more than sixteen victories with the jet fighter was scored with the only usable Me 262 A-1a/U1, the fighter with the mixed armament of MG 151, MK 103 and MK 108 guns.

Above: The Me 262 B-1a two-seater captured at Lechfeld.

Below: In June 1945, these Me 262's were prepared for ferrying to Cherbourg.

Above:
The cockpit of the Me 262 B-1a trainer at Willow Grove.

Upper left:
This Me 262 B-1a was already given American markings at Lechfeld.

Left:
The plane makes an intermediate stop at Melun in the summer of 1945.

Right:
The "White 2", a plane of the EKdo,
stationed at Lechfeld.

Left: The "White 5" was also stationed at Lechfeld.

Jagdgeschwader 7

The reorganization of the Luftwaffe units in the west resulted in long delays in the formation of JG 7. Only in November 1944 did the squadron's history begin. By including the pilots of the former *Kommando Nowotny*, the squadron staff and III. Gruppe were built up quickly. The pilots began to score combat victories, especially in the Berlin area and central Germany. Then came defensive fighting against Allied bomber packs, which appeared in the skies in incredible numbers. In mid-April of 1945 the squadron was formed into JG 7, which had to withdraw to Prague, since the USAAF was attacking the former air bases almost daily from the air and preventing any flying.

I./JG 7 was set up at Kaltenkirchen, near Hamburg. Not until March 1945, though, could the gruppe go into action with thirty Me 262's. The first battles between four-engine bombers and Me 262 A-1a/R1 planes, armed with rockets, over northern Germany brought more than surprising success. In the end, this gruppe was also moved across central Germany to Prague. Along with the pilots of the *Hogeback Gefechtsverband* (Combat Unit), they went into battle again from there and flew successful low-level attacks on the advancing Soviet armies.

II. and IV. Gruppen scarcely existed any more except on paper. In May of 1945 the JV 44 (Galland) was supposed to join the squadron as its fourth gruppe.

In the few months it existed, the JG 7 presumably used the Me 262 to score more than 500 aerial victories. Approximately 3.7 enemy planes were lost for every Me 262 lost.

The "Yellow 8", factory #112385, was captured in central Germany in April, 1945.

Aircraft of JG 7, which saw frequent service
from air bases in the Berlin area.

Above: "White 3" of *Ofhr.* Mutke, who landed in
Switzerland on April 24 because of fuel shortage.

Above: A picture taken by a camera aboard an escort
fighter: Me 262 (upper left) versus B-24.

Left: This Me 262 was captured intact by the Western
Allies.

"Red 1" prepares to take off.

Right: "White 4" was left at Ebendorf, near Magdeburg, when the war ended.

MESSERSCHMITT ME 262

Model	Registration	Factory #	First Flight	Last Use	Notes
Me 262 V1	PC+UA	—	3/27/42	Factory	Crash 6/7/44
Me 262 V2	PC+UB	—	10/1/42	Factory	Crash 4/18/43
Me 262 V3	PC+UC	—	7/17/42	Factory	Air raid 9/44
Me 262 V4	PC+UD	—	5/15/43	Factory	Wreck 7/26/43
Me 262 V5	PC+UE	—	6/7/43	Factory	Crash 2/1/44
Me 262 V6	VI+AA	130001	10/17/43	Factory	Crash 3/8/44
Me 262 V7	VI+AB	130002	12/20/43	Factory	Crash 5/19/44
Me 262 V8	VI+AC	130003	12/15/42	I./KG 51	Combat service
Me 262 V9	VI+AD	130004	1/19/44	Lechfeld*	Flying in 1945
Me 262 V10	VI+AE	130005	4/1/44	EK 262	Flying in 1945
Me 262 S1	VI+AF	130006	March 44	EK 262	Damaged 4/44
Me 262 S2	VI+AG	130007	April 44	EK 262	Damaged 6/44
Me 262 S3	VI+AH	130008	April 44	EK 262	Damaged 4/44
Me 262 S4	VI+AI	130009	May 44	Factory	Damaged 4/44
Me 262 S5	VI+AJ	130010	May 44	Rechlin	Crash 10.8.44
Me 262 S6	VI+AK	130011	May 44	EK 262	Damaged 5/44
Me 262 S7	VI+AL	130012	May 44	?	Leipheim
Me 262 S8	VI+AM	130013	May 44	Factory	Air raid 7/19/44
Me 262 S9	VI+AN	130014	May 44	?	Leipheim
Me 262 S10	VI+AO	130015	May 44	Factory	Flying in 1945
Me 262 S11	VI+AP	130016	May 44	?	Leipheim
Me 262 S12	VI+AQ	130017	May 44	EK 262	Wreck 10/44
Me 262 S13	VI+AR	130018	June 44	Rechlin**	Wreck 10/44
Me 262 S14	VI+AS	130019	June 44	I./KG 51	Combat service
Me 262 S15	VI+AT	130020	June 44	EK 262	Damaged 1/45

* Factory: Messerschmitt AG. Lechfeld: Used at Lechfeld base.
** Leipheim: Built at Leipheim, no other data. Rechlin: Test Center, Rechlin-Larz.

Left:
Side and cutaway views of a Jumo 004 jet engine.

Above and upper right: This plane, factory #501232, belonged to the little-known Industrial Protection Unit (ISS).

Right: "White 3" again, May 1945.

The Galland Fighter Unit · JV 44

In 1944, suitable means of defense against the Allied bomber units had to be found. Along with the assault groups, *General* Galland wanted to come up with a "great strike", using hundreds of fighters against a single bomber group. But after the Operation "Bodenplatte", the necessary aircraft were lacking. Disagreements with Göring became insurmountable after the end of 1944. Adolf Galland was relieved as General der Jagdflieger, and Jagdverband (JV) 44 was established on February 24, 1945. Retraining for the Me 262 could be concluded at the end of March. The unit was transferred to Munich-Riem and flew its missions over southern Germany from there. In the first days of April, pilots of Jagdgeschwadern 2, 6, 7 and 26 and the training units of JG 101 to 105 scored more than seven aerial victories.

On April 9, 1944 an air raid on Riem took place, causing a brief interruption of combat missions. Eleven days later, On April 20, the first Me 262's with R4M racks were ready for action. The B-26 unit that attacked on that day lost half a dozen of its medium bombers. April 26 was the last day on which the service crews could report a noteworthy number of the jets ready for action. Under the capable leadership of *General* Galland and *Major* Bär, five more victories could be scored. After flying missions from the Autobahn, the unit had to withdraw to Salzburg and Innsbruck on May 1, 1945.

During just one month — with very few losses of their own — they were able to score more than 45 aerial victories.

One of the few Me 262 A-1a planes of JV 44, transferred to the Innsbruck area.

Combat Victories of the Me 262

Unit	Scores
Stab and III./JG 7	450
I. and II./JG 7	70
10./NJG 11 (Kommando Welter)	50
Jagdverband 44	55
III.(Replacement)/JG 2	40
IV.(Replacement)/KG 1	5
Kommando Nowotny	25
Test Command 262/Thierfelder Command	10
I. & II./KG(J) 54	15
I. & II./KG 51	5
(Partially estimated)	

Above: This Me 262 A-1a was probably flown by *Oberstleutnant* Bär in JV 44.

Right: This Me 262, factory #111857, was used by JV 44 in Austria in 1945.

High-Speed Fighter

As a constructive basis for the building of new aircraft and for the information of the Air Ministry, the manufacturers supplied so-called "project submissions." The first four project submissions for the Me 262 concerned the submission of the early test models and the later series models. Not until the fifth was a thoroughgoing improvement of the basic design undertaken. Through considerable modifications to the cabin, control surfaces and wings, upgrading to Mach 0.83 was attempted. The first step in this direction was the reequipping of Me 262 V9 as a stage I high-speed fighter, called HG I for short. The model was given the often-mentioned "racing cabin" and a modified rudder with an angle of 40 degrees.

The second high-speed fighter (HG II) was to have this angle changed to 35 degrees, while that of HG III was raised to 45 degrees. The last-named craft would also have looked considerably different from the usual Me 262. The two turbojet engines —according to plan — were set close to the fuselage, and the landing gear was to be moved. The newly reshaped surfaces gave the plane a really sleek appearance and the possibility of attaining operating speeds around 950 kph — so much for the design phase. The actual rebuilding of the Me 262 took months.

Around the beginning of 1945, the new parts for the HG II fighter stood ready at Lechfeld. But before the #111538 plane could make its first flight, the second high-speed fighter was damaged by another jet at Lechfeld. Because parts were lacking, the plane could not be repaired.

The HG III design never went beyond the project stage.

The ninth Me 262 prototype, rebuilt as a high-speed fighter (HG I).

Drawings for the planned HG III fighter.

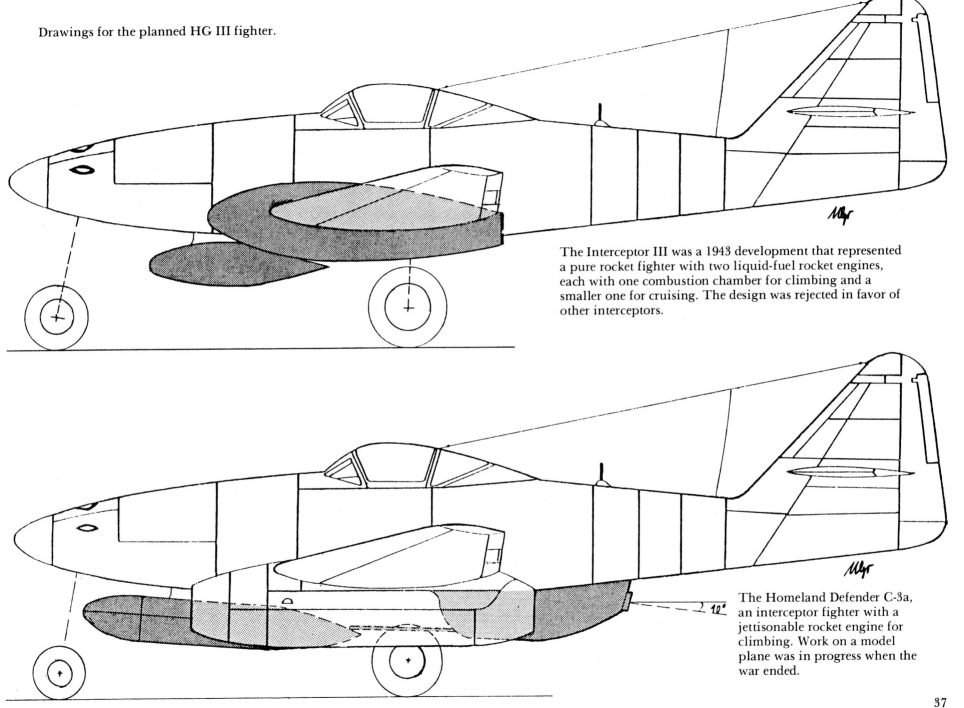

The Interceptor III was a 1943 development that represented a pure rocket fighter with two liquid-fuel rocket engines, each with one combustion chamber for climbing and a smaller one for cruising. The design was rejected in favor of other interceptors.

The Homeland Defender C-3a, an interceptor fighter with a jettisonable rocket engine for climbing. Work on a model plane was in progress when the war ended.

Assault Planes and Pack Destroyers (Sturmflugzeuge and Pulkzerstörer)

During World War II the Luftwaffe steadily increased the calibers of aircraft weapons. The path from the MG 15 led via the MG 151 and MK 108 to the MK 213. But in 1944 the MK 108 was already showing noticeable shortcomings. The armament experts began to consider equipping the Me 262 with different bow weapons. Along with several other fighters with mixed armament, the Me 262 A-4, the later A-1a/U1, was developed.

As happened to many production runs, the war's events allowed only one model to be finished in 1945. When more powerful engines finally became ready for series production, the six-barrel bow turret of MK 108 guns (A-1a/U5) was again taken up. In addition, the designers set out to put the probably best-armed Me 262 A into action.

This was a plane with four MK 213/30 guns plus 24 R4M launchers.

As of the summer of 1943, the BK 5 cannon was installed in several Messerschmitt 410's. This gun was to be installed in the Arado Ar 234 as of December 1944, as well as in the Me 262. On December 15, 1944 a basic decision in this area was made. After it had been seen that the MK 112/412 could not be used for the time being and the BK 5 could not be considered, the MK 214 was now to be installed in the jet fighters. Hitler himself advocated this on January 20, 1945. The first firing tests, on February 28, 1945, inspired justified hopes. The fuselage nose with the MK 214V2 arrived at Oberammergau on March 11 to be installed in the cell of #111899. This was the

first Me 262 A-1a/U4. By March 21 the pack destroyer had made a total of 19 flights. In early April, a second plane was ready, and *Major* Herget attacked a pack of B-26 bombers with it on April 16, 1945.

At the beginning of 1945 the age of the rocket-armed jet fighter also began to take concrete shape. After the first tests of two WGr 21 launchers on the fuselage, carried out by *Major* Sinner of the III./JG 7, the R4M rockets gained more and more importance. The launching racks developed by *Hauptmann* Kiefer were tested at Parchim in the spring of 1945. The target, a Savoia SM 81, was reduced to scrap metal.

The opened gun housing and the modified landing gear of the Me 262 A-1a/ U4 are shown in this photo, taken in the summer of 1945.

Left page: Factory #170083, one of the two pack destroyers, after its arrival in Melun, France.

II./JG 7 was the first unit to receive the R4M rockets. On March 19, 1945 they were first used. The combat unit of JG 7 shot down more than six four-engine bombers of an Allied flight.

A second rocket, the Kramer X-4, was almost ready for series production in 1945. It was a wire-controlled projectile that, according to a proposal of December 20, 1944, could be launched from one of up to six launching rails under the Me 262. A test from Me 262 A-1a #111994 on a captured B-24 proved the destructive power of this air-to-air rocket. The development of other special weapons was never finished.

The Armored Plane I/II was planned as a special means of fighting bomber packs effectively. As with the very successful Fw 190 assault (sturm) fighters, the cell of the Me 262 was to be heavily armored. The take-off weight thus was increased to 7300 kilograms. It was to be armed with four WGr 21 launchers as well as four MK 108 guns. Because of the greater weight, though, the flight time of this version was reduced by about 25%. Models were presumably under construction at the end of 1944, but the downgraded performance made their actual use seem pointless.

Preparing to take off at Lechfeld in 1945.

Me 262 Production Types

Me 262 A-1a	Jet fighter with two Jumo 004B engines
Me 262 A-1b	Jet fighter with two BMW 003A engines
Me 262 A-1a/R1	Jet plane like A-1a plus R4M rockets
Me 262 A-1a/Bo	Makeshift blitz bomber
Me 262 A-1a/U1	Jet fighter with mixed weapons: two each MK 103, MK 108 and MG 151 (planned production version)
Me 262 A-1a/U2	Bad-weather fighter with FuG 125 radar
Me 262 A-1a/U3	Unarmed reconnaissance plane rebuilt from A-1a
Me 262 A-1a/U4	Heavy jet fighter with MK 214 guns
Me 262 A-1a/U4	Heavy jet fighter with six MK 108 in nose
Me 262 A-2a	Blitz bomber with only two MK 108 guns
Me 262 A-2a/R2	Blitz bomber with heavier armor
Me 262 A-2a/U1	Blitz bomber with TSA equipment
Me 262 A-2a/U2	Two-seat highest-speed bomber (Lotfe bomber)
Me 262 A-3a	Armored Plane I and II
Me 262 A-4a	Number intended for reconnaissance Me 262 A-1a/U3 and A-1a/U1 fighter with mixed weapons
Me 262 A-5a	Armed reconnaissance plane
Me 262 B-1a	Two-seat trainer
Me 262 B-1a/U1	Two-seat makeshift night fighter
Me 262 B-2a	Two-seat night fighter with Jumo 004B engines

Me 262 C-1a	Interceptor with two Jumo 004B and one Hans Walter Kiel (HWK) engines: Homeland Defender I
Me 262 C-2b	Interceptor with two BMW 003R engines: Homeland Defender II
Me 262 C-3a	Interceptor with two Jumo 004B and one HWK in the fuselage
Me 262 D-1	Number intended for Me 262 C-2b

Me 262 E-1	Number intended for Me 262 A-1a/U4
Me 262 S	Zero-series model of Me 262 A-1a
Me 262 V	Test model of Me 262
Me 262 W	Number intended for Me 262 with Pulso jet power

Below: Drawing from a proposal describing additional uses of the Me 262.

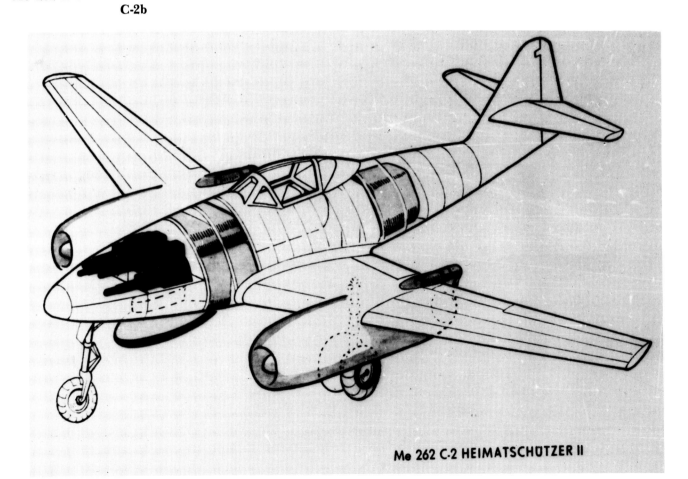

Me 262 C-2 HEIMATSCHÜTZER II

Me 262 C - The Interceptors

The Me 262 interceptors belong to an area of German aircraft history of which very little is known to date.

As early as April of 1941 there were important discussions concerning the project with auxiliary rocket propulsion. The use of HWK units were to give the later jet fighters the ability to take action successfully against high-altitude bombers and in object protection.

But it was not until July 20, 1943 that the project description of Interceptor I (a plane with the RII 211/3 rocket engine in its tail) could be presented to the Air Ministry.

To build a model, the Me 262 A-1a, factory #130186 was used. After the fuel system and the third engine were installed, numerous test runs began. The system was improved step by step. A setback was caused by damage to the fuel system on January 29, 1945. After repairs, *Major* Heinz Bär made the first flight on February 15, 1945. In just 2.5 minutes the first Me 262 C-1a — with rocket assistance — climbed from 6000 to 14,700 meters. The official first flight was made on February 27 by factory pilot G. Lindner, who climbed to 8000 meters over Lechfeld in three minutes. By March 22 the plane had made six flights; it was later damaged by low-flying Allied planes and was not repaired.

The second special version was the Me 262 C-1b interceptor, which had two rocket engines installed on its BMW 003 powerplants. As with Interceptor I, the development of the auxiliary power system took up much time. The project description of September and the first discussions of November 1943 were followed by an endless series of test-bench runs and experiments. Finally, on December 20, 1944, a first model plane, factory #170074, was rebuilt.

Constant problems with the fuel system and the two powerplants delayed the work considerably. On January 25, 1945 the right combustion chamber exploded, on February 21 the left auxiliary motor burned out, and leaks in the fuel lines and engine changes followed. Finally, on March 23, 1945, it was ready. A final test run took place without additional problems. The first flight ensued on March 26, 1945. With a climbing speed of about 120 meters per second, the second Homeland Defender climbed to 8200 meters in only 1.5 minutes. Three days later, Messerschmitt made a second and last test flight at Lechfeld. The TLR (engine with rocket assistance) testing then had to be halted on orders from above.

Still to be mentioned is the Homeland Defender III or the Me 262 C-3a, a plane with a jettisonable rocket engine and two 600-liter drop tanks. The construction of this model was likewise halted at the end of March 1945. Professor Sänger also worked on jet ducts that could be attached to the Jumo 004 engine.

Although all these projects were far superior to the Me 163, readiness for series production was never attained, as the new technology could not be mastered within a short time.

The first and only Me 262 C-1a, a fast-climbing interceptor.

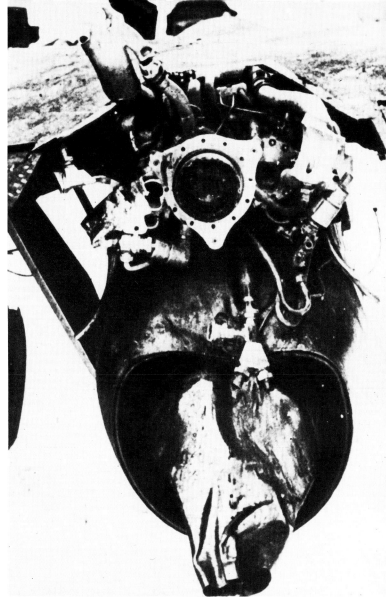

Above:
The destroyed TLR engine and damaged wing.

Left:
The engine of the Me 262 C-2b explodes at Lechfeld on February 25, 1945.

First Jet Night Fighters

After the heavy thousand-bomber attacks, and with the beginning of the aerial battle around Berlin, the numbers of British Mosquito flights increased strongly since 1943. The search for a really superior night fighter began. The path to the high-performance Ar 234 B-2/N "Nightingale" (Nachtigall) night fighter, though, turned out to be a dead-end street. The rebuilding of Me 262 B-1a trainers, on the other hand, offered other possibilities. But only in November of 1944 did the Air Ministry approve the production of the Me 262 B-1a/U1 makeshift night fighter. The production of these machines was planned to take place in two stages:
— The Me 262 A-1a single-seat night fighter with FuG 350Z, and
— The B-1a/U1 two-seater with FuG 218 as the second interim solution, until the Me 262 B-2a became reality.

On November 21, 1944 the mockup was examined and basically approved.

In mid-February of 1945, series rebuilding took place at the Lufthansa works in Berlin-Staaken. The night fighters bore factory numbers 110305, 110306, 110630, 110375, 110378 and 111980. The first of these planes was sent to the test center at Rechlin and then to the 10./NJG 11. This unit had been developed from a one-man jet night-fighter unit by *Olt.* Kurt Welter on February 28, 1945. It began in December 1944, when two new test commands were set up, one with the Ar 234 and one with the Messerschmitt jet fighter. OKL had chosen Kurt Welter to command the Me 262 unit. Just a few days later, on December 12, 1944, he scored his first night-fighter victory with the Me 262 A-1a. In early January 1945, he shot down two Mosquitos, plus several Lancaster bombers a short time later. On March 22, the German jet night fighters scored a success that still remains unique. Five DH Mosquitos were defeated in aerial combat. It is especially noteworthy that none of the Me 262 A-1a planes used was equipped with a night-sight device or radar set. The pilots simply used the normal day fighter version with slightly modified instruments. The only single-seater with the FuG 218 device, #170056, was usually used for testing purposes and thus hardly ever saw action.

Another Me 262 of the Welter unit, "Red 4", even had angled MG 151 guns behind the cabin.

Only when the Me 262 B-1a/U1 was available did radar-supported night fighting begin. Constant technical disturbances, especially with the fuel system, allowed the B-1a/U1 to take part in

The Me 262 A-1a night-fighter test plane, factory number 170056, after crash-landing early in 1945. Note the two radar antennas in the wings.

combat only five times before the war ended. In the process, though, its pilots, including *Olt.* Welter, shot down several DH Mosquitos.

In mid-March the 10./NJG 11's fuel reserves ran dangerously low. In the ensuing weeks the pilots also flew low-level attacks with the Me 262.

In the five months of its existence, *Kommando Welter* and the 10./NJG 11 scored some fifty aerial victories in seventy missions. Mosquitos alone accounted for 35 of them. Kurt Welter scored more than 25 victories with the Me 262 and thus became Germany's most successful jet pilot.

Although it was hardly possible in 1945 to even think of building a greatly improved night fighter on the basis of the Me 262, designing went on quietly. The first production Me 262 B-2a plane was supposed to have been finished in mid-April, a few days before the Metallbau AG Offingen's factory was captured. Other night fighters with HeS 11 or PTL (propeller-turbine) engines and Bremen-O radar were never built.

Above:
One of *Kommando Welter*'s (10./NJG 11) interim night fighters with British markings.

Right:
Former "Red 10" of the 10./ NJG 11 at St. Dizier.

Short-Range Reconnaissance

Jet reconnaissance planes were already being designed by Messerschmitt in 1941. But only in June of 1943 did the *General der Aufklärerprojekte* (Reconnaissance) express himself in favor of these fast planes. Reconnaissance Projects I, Ia and II followed. Since series production of the Me 262 had to be waited for, only suggestions and designs resulted. The first interim reconnaissance plane (Me 262 A-1a/U3) was created in the summer of 1944 from #170006 and equipped with two Rb 50/30 serial cameras in the nose.

Under the leadership of *Hauptmann* Braunegg, who bore the Knight's Cross, the combat testing command was set up. Some of his reconnaissance aircraft were already equipped with an MK 108 machine cannon as a makeshift defensive weapon. It was installed in the very tip of the fuselage nose.

Late in the summer of 1944 the whole Short-Range Reconnaissance Group (Nahaufklärungsgruppe) 6 was to be reequipped with the Me 262. By January of 1945, though, only four jet planes had reached NAG 6; the *Kommando Braunegg* also received some planes. Finally the test unit was absorbed by the 2./NAG 6, which strengthened the gruppe. More than fifty tactical reconnaissance missions were then flown over western Europe alone, providing valuable information about their own conduct. Some of the flights extended over southern England. In addition, a mixed combat command — consisting of Ar 234 B-1 and Me 262 A-1a/Ue planes — operated from northern Italy.

By April of 1945 the NAG 6, despite all its efforts, possessed only a third of the aircraft it was supposed to have, though some 35 Me 262's had been reequipped for reconnaissance. Some of them were lost in air raids, and the last planes were captured by Allied troops at Lechfeld at the war's end.

Above: Colonel Watson's command gathers before one of the jet reconnaissance planes for a last photo. Below: Lechfeld, June 10, 1945. Among the men are Karl Baur and Ludwig Hofmann.

TECHNICAL DATA

Model	Me 262 A-1a	Me 262 B-2a	Me 262 C-1a
Use	fighter	night fighter	interceptor
Crew	1	2	1
Wingspan meters	12.501	12.501	12.501
Length (meters)	10.605	11.752	10.605
Height (meters)	2.850	2.850	2.850
Track (meters)	2.550	2.550	2.550
Wing surface (sq.m.)	21,700	21,700	21,700
Dry weight (kg)	4,364	4,760	4,550
Flying weight (kg)	6,938	7,700	8,195
Top speed (kph)	870 at 6 km	785 at 6 km	885 (- rockets)
Top speed (kph)	865 at 9 km	710 at 9 km	990 at 12 km
Climbing to 6 (km)	6.80 min.	10.00 min.	2.55 min.
Climbing to 9 (km)	13.00 min.	17.80 min.	4.08 min.
Flying time (min.)	70	145	40 at 12 km
Range (km)	960	1300	745 at 12 km
Service ceiling (m)	11,450	10,500	12,000+

Me 262 TEST AIRCRAFT

Werk.Num.	Registration	Testing Assignments	Model
110484	+	Lotfe cabin, course control	A-2a/U2
110555	+	Lotfe cabin II, navigation	A-2a/U2
111355	+	Weapon system with 6 MK 108	A-1a/U5
111538	+	High-speed fighter	HG II
111857	+	Improved production model	–
111899	+	Weapon system with MK 214	A-1a/U4
111994	+	Rocket launcher 21, R 100	A-1a
130018	E3+01	Engine tests (Jumo)	A-1a
130170	+	Engine tests (BMW)	A-1b
130163	E2+01	Landing gear tests	A-1a
130164	WA+TA	Weapons & TSA tests	A-1a
130165	E4+E5	Hydraulic & FT tests	A-1a
130167	SQ+WF	Jettisonable tanks, brakes	A-1a
130168	E3+02	High-altitude engine tests	A-1a
130170	E2+02	Performance tests	A-1a
130172	EK+L1	Fuel & tire tests	A-1a
130174	EK+L2	Long-term tests	A-1a
130175	+	General flight tests	A-1a
130186	+	Homeland Defender I	C-1a
130188	E7+01	Diving sight, BZA, TSA	A-1a
130189	+	Flight tests	A-1a
170038	E3+03	Engine tests (Junkers)	A-1a
170039	EK+L3	Long-term engine tests	A-1a
170056	+	Take-off aid, FuG 218, 226	A-1a
170057	WA+02	Weapon tests	A-1a
170070	E7+02	TSA, drop tests	A-1a
170074	+	Homeland Defender II	C-2b
170078	+	Engine tests (BMW)	A-1b
170079	+	Wheel drive tests	A-1a
170083	+	MK 214, taxiing tests	A-1a/U4
170086	+	Stability, Jettisonable tanks	A-1a
170095	+	Landing gear, night tests	A-1a
170303	+	Drop tests to 1000 kg	A-1a
170394	+	General flight tests	A-1a